# HOW TO DRESS FOR WOMEN

How To Look Elegant, Classy, Stylish, Charming Chic, And Beautiful Every Day

Madison Styles

Copyright © Madison Styles, 2023. All rights reserved.

This publication and its contents are protected by copyright laws and international treaties. No part of this publication may be reproduced or transmitted in any form or by any means, electronic or mechanical, including photocopying, recording or any information storage and retrieval system, without prior permission in writing from the copyright holder.

# TABLE OF CONTENTS

**INTRODUCTION**..............................................................6
**Part I: The Foundations of Elegance**........................ 11
   1. The Power of Personal Style............................... 11
   2. Bringing Out Your Elegance Within.................... 14
   3. The Basics of a Versatile Wardrobe for Every Woman................................................................. 17
**Part II: Mastering Different Styles**............................ 26
   4. The Art of Dressing Classy: Redefining Timeless Elegance................................................................27
   5. Dressing for Success with Ease: Professional Style......................................................................32
   6. Expensive Chic: Embracing Luxury and Sophistication....................................................... 36
   7. Sensual Sophistication: Unleashing Your Sexy Confidence.............................................................41
   8. Honoring Cultural Attire by Adorning Traditional Beauty...................................................................46
   9. The Fusion of Cross-Cultural Couture for the Modern Woman...................................................... 49
**Part III: How to Dress for Every Situation**................ 54
   10. Day-to-Day Chic: Adding Style to Your Casual Clothes..................................................................55
   11. Glamorous Evenings: Dressing to Dazzle........ 58
   12. Wonders of the Wedding: Choosing the Ideal Guest Attire............................................................ 63
   13. Cocktail Attire: How to Dress Perfectly and Fabulously............................................................. 66
   14. A Walk Down the Aisle: Bridal Elegance and

Beyond..............................................................................71

**Part IV: Dressing Through the Seasons................... 77**

15. Effortless Style for Blooming Days: Spring Splendor............................................................... 77

16. Embracing Heat with Grace in the Summer..... 81

17. The Allure of Autumn: Stunning Fall Fashion... 86

18. Cozy Clothing for Cold Days from Winter Wonders................................................................ 89

**Part V: Dressing with Confidence............................ 94**

19. The Confidence Effect: Your Empowerment via Clothes................................................................. 95

20. Promoting body positivity by embracing each curve..................................................................... 98

21. The Magic of Accessories: Adding Elegance to Any Look............................................................ 103

22. Sustainable Fashion: Making Sense of the Industry............................................................... 107

23. Dressing for Different Body Types to Boost Confidence.......................................................... 111

**Part VI: Beyond Clothing........................................ 116**

24. The Art of Makeup: Enhancing Your Natural Beauty................................................................. 117

25. Finding Your Signature Hairstyle with Hair Mastery............................................................... 120

26. The Power of Fragrance: The Style Statement of Perfume............................................................... 125

27. Elevate with Aromas: Picking the Best Body Sprays, Deodorants, and Perfumes...................... 129

**Part VII: Navigating Fashion Trends...................... 132**

28. Using High Fashion in Your Wardrobe: Decoding Runway Trends.................................................... 133

29. Vintage Revival: Integrating Classic Pieces into Contemporary Looks.................................................. 136

30. Style Evolution: Adapting Your Wardrobe with Changing Trends.................................................. 142

**Part VIII Exploring the World of Accessories........ 149**

31. How to Choose, Layer, and Mix Pieces of Jewelry..............................................................150

32. Hats & Headwear: A Touch of Elegance.........153

33. Bags and Beyond: Finding the Ideal Handbag for Every Look..............................................................157

34. The Art of Scarves: Stylish and Versatile Accessorizing Ideas................................................162

35. Shoe Symphony: Finding the Perfect Pair of Heels and Flats......................................................165

**Part IX: Embracing Personal Expression............... 170**

36. Tapping into Your Inner Muse: How to Dress with Confidence and Authenticity................................. 171

37. Honoring Cultural Traditions: Combining History with Modern Design................................................. 174

38. Custom Creations: Designing Your Own Clothing and Accessories................................................. 178

39. Your ongoing style evolution: The Fashion Journey.................................................................. 181

**Conclusion: An Elegant and Self-Assured Journey... 186**

**HAPPY DRESSING.................................................. 190**

# INTRODUCTION

Meet Freda, a friend of mine who used to struggle with the constant worry of "What should I wear?" For her, it wasn't a little issue; it was a daily conundrum that sapped her self-confidence and dimmed her normally vivacious personality. The stress of picking the appropriate clothes appeared to consume her thoughts whether she was getting ready for professional meetings, social events, or even informal outings. Freda's attire has changed from being a means of self-expression and creativity to a source of worry.

Little did she realize that this book was about to change her approach to fashion and transform her life in ways she never dreamed of until, one day, in the midst of her aggravation, I shared with her a copy of "How To Dress For Women: The Ultimate Guide to Women's Fashion Mastery."

The book's deep insights caught Freda's attention as she read through its pages. She learned the importance of embracing her particular style instead of being told what to wear, giving her a way to express her genuine self without boundaries. She learned how to dress for many situations, whether it was leading the room in formal settings or exuding beauty at nighttime parties. She waded through the jungle of seasonal trends using the book as a guide, selecting clothing that reflected her true self.

But the book focused on the power of confidence rather than just the clothes. Freda came to understand that her clothes weren't simply for concealing up; they were also a declaration of her confidence. She noticed that she was standing a little straighter and making eye contact with a newfound sense of elegance as she accepted body acceptance and the advice on using makeup to enhance her appearance.

Freda's path involved a significant change in her perspective as well as good clothing. She realized that clothes were an artistic medium and an expression of her uniqueness that could alter her mood, affect her interactions, and bring joy into her life. With her newly acquired knowledge, she went through each day feeling more empowered, embracing the woman she was, and radiating captivating confidence.

"How To Dress For Women" develops into a thorough manual in the ensuing chapters, weaving together a complex tapestry of disclosures, tips, and tactics. This book is more than just a how-to guide; it's a call to adventure. A journey where clothing is not a duty but a celebration, where the mirror becomes a reflection of your inner strength and beauty, and where fashion is a tool through which you paint your personality on the canvas of life.

This book is your dependable companion for everything from comprehending the subtleties of various styles to overcoming the difficulties of dressing for every event and season. It serves as a guide for changing your outfit, making it reflect your ideals, and perfecting the self-expression technique. The pages that follow provide the keys to unlocking your fashion potential, regardless of whether you're looking for timelessly elegant, professional sophistication, sensual attractiveness, or a cross-cultural fusion of trends.

The transformation you will experience inside these pages is only somewhat hinted at by Freda's story. As you read through the upcoming chapters, keep in mind that this trip is about appreciating your uniqueness rather than trying to fit in. It's about letting go of the restrictions imposed by fashion standards and discovering freedom in expressing your individuality. It's about improving your life in the long run—in terms of confidence, style, and life.

Come along with me as we set out on this journey of authenticity, beauty, and empowerment. Let "How To Dress For Women" serve as your road map through the world of women's fashion, enabling you to enter the spotlight with poise, self-expression, and confidence. Your journey has just begun.

# Part I: The Foundations of Elegance

## 1. The Power of Personal Style

Personal style is a language that you use to express your identity, values, and feelings to the outside world. It is not simply about the things you wear. It offers the chance to create a visual narrative that expresses who you are without using words. Your individual sense of style is your mark on the world of fashion—a distinguishing characteristic that reflects who you really are.

Embracing your unique sense of style goes beyond simply following fashion trends or emulating runway appearances. It's about self-discovery, a reflective process that explores your preferences, experiences, and goals. The seasons of your life and the many chapters of your life's tale influence how your personal style changes as you do.

As you develop your own sense of style, you gain newfound power. Your choice of clothing serves as a tool to boost your self-esteem, improve your mood, and make a lasting impression. Your unique style is a fluid mirror of your inner self that changes to fit the situation and your emotions. It's a daily practice that enables you to recognize the woman you are becoming and celebrate your uniqueness as a form of self-care.

## 2. Bringing Out Your Elegance Within

Elegance is a state of being that springs from your self-assurance, kindness, and confidence rather than just being a physical quality. Discovering your inner elegance is a life-changing adventure that transcends fashion and affects all facets of your existence.

A mindset of confidence in one's values and self-respect is what is meant by elegance. It's about accepting your flaws and eccentricities and realizing that your shortcomings are what make you incredibly special. When you conduct yourself with inner grace, you exude a sense of composure that enthralls people who are in your vicinity.

While your outside appearance can be improved by your wardrobe, the actual definition of elegance is found in the way you hold yourself, how you treat other people, and the sense of genuineness you portray. It's a blend of confidence and flair that creates harmony between your inner and exterior worlds and leaves a lasting impression.

It takes self-reflection, self-compassion, and a dedication to growth to reveal your inner grace. It entails letting go of self-doubt and accepting self-love. As you set out on this road, keep in mind that elegance is a daily practice—a decision to respect your essence and exude grace in every connection.

We'll explore further the subtleties of individual style and inner elegance throughout this book. By leading you through exercises that engage your intuition and help you create a wardrobe that reflects your genuine self, we'll examine strategies to help you discover your individual fashion identity. We'll also explore the discipline of developing inner elegance, providing you with knowledge and techniques that will enable you to carry yourself with assurance, kindness, and a captivating charm.

The concepts of inner elegance and personal style are not esoteric ideas reserved for the privileged; rather, they are achievable and empowering states of being that you may embrace and embody as you read the pages that follow. Here is where the path to realizing your inner elegance and stylish potential begins. Together, let's go out on this journey of self-discovery and development, embracing your uniqueness and radiating the grace that exists inside you.

## 3. The Basics of a Versatile Wardrobe for Every Woman

A diverse wardrobe is the basis for carefree and fashionable wearing. A variety of costumes can be easily put together thanks to the carefully chosen elements that flow from one event to the next. Building a diverse wardrobe is a purposeful and thoughtful process that builds the groundwork for self-assured and innovative dressing, rather than simply amassing clothing.

## 3.1 The Fundamental Elements of a Versatile Wardrobe

Before getting into the precise necessities, let's look at the fundamental ideas that guide a varied wardrobe:

### 3.1.1 Quality Priority Over Quantity

Invest in durable, well-made items. They will last a lifetime. The need for continual replacement is decreased by the lifespan and durability provided by high-quality textiles and craftsmanship.

### 3.1.2 Classical pieces with modern touches

Strike a balance between pieces that are motivated by trends and timeless classics. The foundation of your wardrobe should consist of timeless pieces like a white button-down shirt, well-fitting jeans, and a tailored blazer, while fashionable accessories give it a modern, fresh feel.

### 3.1.3 Potential for Combination

Your wardrobe should have a variety of pieces that may be worn together and separately. Being versatile means being able to put together numerous looks using a small amount of accessories.

### 3.1.4 An impartial base

An adaptable wardrobe's base is made up of neutral hues. Bolder colors and patterns can be included in designs using adaptable backdrops of black, white, gray, navy, and beige.

### 3.1.5 Flexibility in Occasion

Depending on the occasion, choose clothing that may be dressed up or down. Casual brunches and formal gatherings should be seamlessly transitioned by adaptable clothing.

## 3.2 Wardrobe Requirements

### 3.2.1 A traditional white shirt

An absolute must is a pristine white shirt. Its adaptability has no bounds; layer it under a blazer for a refined combination, slip it into a pencil skirt for the office, or wear it with jeans for a casual approach.

### 3.2.2 The Little Black Dress (LBD)

The LBD is a staple piece for every woman's wardrobe since it is timeless and universally attractive. Pick a length that can be worn up or down and a silhouette that complements your body type.

### 3.2.3 Jeans That Fit Right

A pair of well-fitting jeans is a wardrobe mainstay. From casual to semi-formal, jeans may be dressed in a variety of ways, whether they are slim, straight, or bootcut.

### 3.2.4 Blazer with a tailored fit

An ensemble is quickly elevated by a fitted blazer, making it appropriate for the workplace, dinner dates, or even a night out. Choose a neutral hue like gray, black, or navy.

### 3.2.5 Neutral trench coat

A neutral trench coat embodies classic elegance. It is ideal for transitional weather and adds refinement to any outfit.

### 3.2.6 Simple shirts and tops

Invest in good basic T-shirts and blouses in muted hues. These can be matched with a variety of bottoms and act as the foundation for layering.

### 3.2.7 Multipurpose Skirt

Pick a skirt that can be dressed up or down for various occasions. An adaptable choice is a neutral-colored midi skirt.

### 3.2.8 Comfortable Flats

Flats that are cozy are necessary for daily wear. Choose footwear that can be worn with dresses, skirts, or pants, like loafers or ballerina flats.

### 3.2.9 Vintage Pumps

Any ensemble quickly gains shine with a pair of timeless shoes. For comfort and adaptability, go with a model that has a moderate heel height.

### 3.2.10 Customized Pants

To look polished and professional, you must wear well-fitting tailored pants. Choose neutral hues like navy, gray, or black.

### 3.2.11 Accessory Statements

Include a couple of standout pieces of jewelry or a multipurpose scarf. These accessories may make an ordinary outfit into a beautiful set.

## 3.3 Choosing Clothing That Is Versatile

Building a diverse wardrobe is a process that takes time and thought. Make a list of the items in your present wardrobe and note any holes that need to be filled. Prioritize quality above quantity while you're shopping, and choose goods that suit your lifestyle and sense of fashion.

Keep in mind that these necessities are the cornerstones of countless outfit combinations as you develop your adaptable wardrobe. You may easily create outfits that suit diverse situations, seasons, and moods by thoughtfully mixing and matching.

Having access to the resources to put together fashionable outfits that express your individual identity gives you the courage to go out in public. You can embrace fashion as a means of self-expression because the worry of "having nothing to wear" is gone. Let your diverse wardrobe serve as the blank canvas on which you paint your authentic style and exhibit your inner elegance as we progress on our journey of fashion mastery.

# Part II: Mastering Different Styles

# 4. The Art of Dressing Classy: Redefining Timeless Elegance

Aesthetically, classiness is timeless and unaffected by fads and trends. Its polished minimalism, flawless tailoring, and understated grace define the look. Developing an inner sense of sophistication and embracing a classic-inspired wardrobe is key to mastering the art of looking smart.

## 4.1 Components of Elegant Attire

### 4.1.1 Simple lines and tailored design

Clean lines and well-tailored silhouettes define classy clothing. Perfectly fitting clothing should highlight your body's natural proportions and give off an image of effortlessness.

### 4.1.2 A subdued color scheme

A sophisticated wardrobe is built on neutral hues like black, white, navy, beige, and gray.

These hues offer a flexible foundation on which you can create your chic combinations.

### 4.1.3 Classic Works

Invest in classic pieces that will last a lifetime. The essentials of stylish clothing are a timeless trench coat, a tailored blazer, a little black dress, and well-fitted trousers.

### 3.1.4 Less is more and minimalism

Decide on quality above quantity to embrace simplicity. Choose carefully chosen pieces for your capsule wardrobe that you can mix and match with ease.

### 4.2 Elegant Styling Advice

### 4.2.1 Equilibrium and Ratio

Make an effort to dress with proportion and balance. For a harmonious silhouette when wearing a fitted shirt, team it with wide-legged pants or a flared skirt.

## 4.2.2 Carefully accessorize

Choose sleek and subtle accessories that enhance your look without drawing attention to it. Perfect options are a delicate bracelet, a string of pearls, or plain stud earrings.

### 4.2.3 Fashionable Footwear

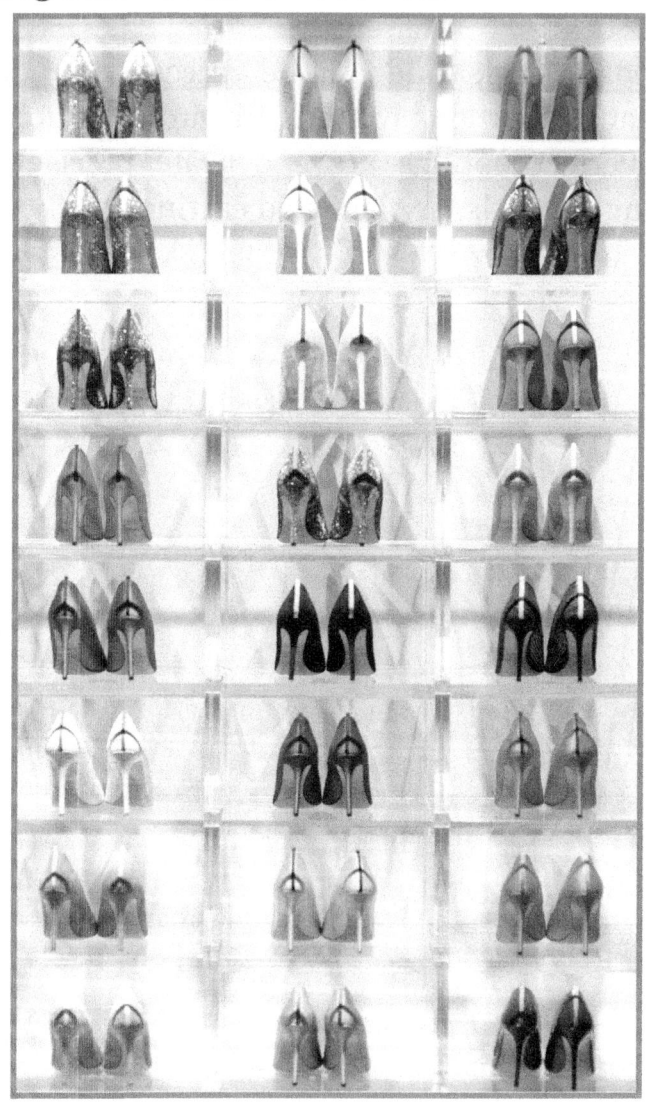

Select sophisticated footwear like ankle boots, loafers, or classic pumps. These classic looks will subtly improve your overall appearance.

### 4.2.4 Traditional makeup and hairstyles

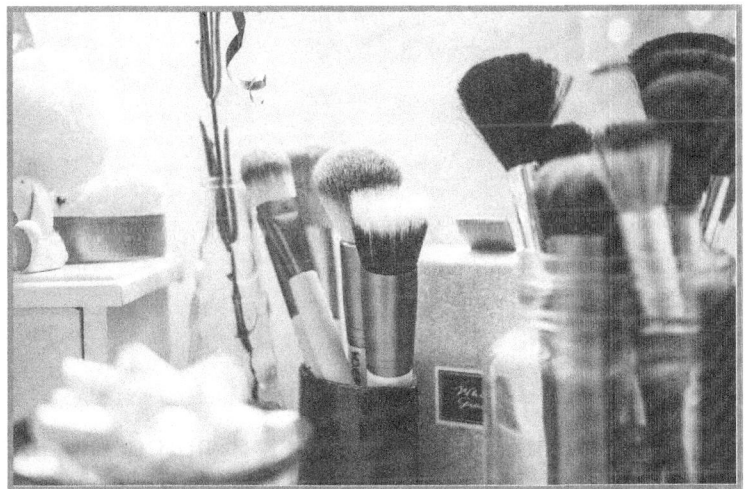

Accept traditional hairstyles like gentle waves, a low ponytail, or a tidy bun. Concentrate on a polished and natural makeup style that highlights your characteristics.

# 5. Dressing for Success with Ease: Professional Style

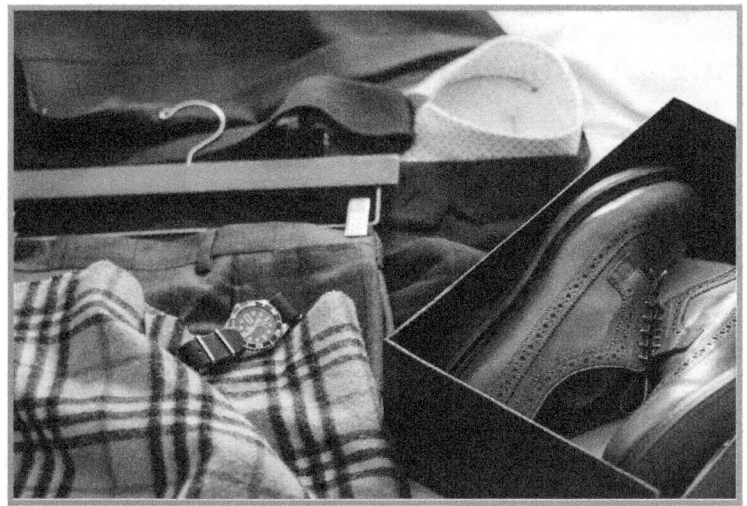

A key weapon for conveying skill, authority, and ambition is your professional style. Beyond simply following a dress code, effortless professional dressing is building a wardrobe that gives you the confidence and poise to take charge of any situation.

## 5.1 Getting the Look

### 5.1.1 Tailored separates and power suits

Invest in well-fitted power suits or neutral-toned separates for mixing and matching. These pieces radiate authority and show that you are up for any task.

### 5.1.2 Traditional shirts and blouses

For a professional outfit, a well-fitting shirt or a traditional button-down blouse are essential pieces. They go perfectly with skirts, pants, and suits.

### 5.1.3 Skirts and Dresses That Reach the Knee

For a sophisticated and businesslike appearance, choose dresses and skirts that are knee-length. For long days at the office, choose comfy outfits.

## 5.2 Successful Styling

### 5.2.1 Colors that Promote Confidence

Dress professionally by including self-assured hues like navy, black, gray, and deep burgundy.

These colors scream authority and demand attention.

### 5.2.2 Paying Close Attention

Pay close attention to little particulars like grooming, footwear, and accessories. Your professional image is enhanced by a distinctive necklace, a sleek briefcase, and well-groomed nails.

### 5.2.3 Structured Bags

Choose structured handbags that radiate class and utility. Pick sizes that allow you to wear your essentials for work without looking bulky.

### 5.2.4 Stylish and Comfy Footwear

Comfort and style should coexist in professional footwear. Select supportive shoes for your feet on busy days, such as closed-toe pumps or loafers.

# 6. Expensive Chic: Embracing Luxury and Sophistication

Regardless of your financial situation, embracing pricey chic means emulating elegance and sophistication. With its meticulously chosen items and meticulous attention to detail, this look emanates grandeur and elegance.

## 6.1 Adding Class to Your Wardrobe

### 6.1.1 Investment Items

Place a higher priority on investments with long-term value. These could include classic jewelry, well-made shoes, and designer handbags.

### 6.1.2 Premium Fabrics and Materials

For a hint of luxury, opt for textiles like silk, cashmere, and premium wool. Pieces that are well-made feel luxurious and last longer.

### 6.1.3 Customization and Tailoring

Spend money on tailoring to make sure your apparel fits well. Customization enables you to add your own touches to your clothing, boosting the overall richness of your appearance.

## 6.2 How to Style the Pricey Chic Look

### 6.2.1 Elegance in one Color

Try wearing monochromatic attire in opulent, rich colors. One hue worn from head to toe makes a classy and eye-catching statement.

### 6.2.2 Statement-making Accessories

Choose accessories with a big impact by making a statement. Your appearance might be completely changed by a bold necklace, a big bracelet, or a pair of striking earrings.

### 6.2.3 Structured and Customized Pieces

Select items that are structured and designed to highlight your figure. A sheath dress, pencil skirt, or blazer that fits nicely radiates sophistication.

### 6.2.4 Luxurious Outerwear

Invest in opulent clothing, such as a trench coat made of wool or cashmere. The first thing people see is your outerwear, so pick pieces that stand out.

Embracing pricey chic is about developing an appreciation for quality, craftsmanship, and attention to detail rather than showing off your wealth. You may develop an opulent and sophisticated look that shows your discriminating taste by making investments in classic pieces, focusing on high-quality fabrics, and building a wardrobe that oozes luxury.

We'll look at how to adopt and personalize these designs in the pages that follow. The tips and tricks offered will help you on your quest to master various looks, whether you're drawn to the timeless elegance of classy clothing, hoping to rule the professional world with an easy style, or looking to add a dash of luxury to your appearance. As you negotiate the complexities of fashion, keep in mind that your sense of style is a window into your inner self and a platform for expressing your identity, self-assurance, and uniqueness.

# 7. Sensual Sophistication: Unleashing Your Sexy Confidence

Sensual sophistication is a look that encourages you to accept your body with charm and confidence while also celebrating your natural sexuality. It's about showcasing your inherent beauty, radiating confidence, and letting your personal style reflect your magnetic personality.

## 7.1 Embracing Sensual Elements

### 7.1.1 Flattering Silhouettes

Select silhouettes that appreciate your contours and emphasize your best features. You can enhance your seductive appeal by wearing bodycon dresses, form-fitting shirts, and fitted bottoms.

### 7.1.2 Necklines and Slits

Choose necklines with a hint of intrigue, including off-the-shoulder, a plunging V-neck, or a sweetheart. Dresses and skirts with high slits can have a dramatic effect.

### 7.1.3 Details Inspired by Lingerie

Dress in lingerie-inspired components including lace, satin, and sheer materials. Your outfit gains a sensuous depth from these small accents.

### 7.1.4 Vibrant Accessory

Select items that command attention and express confidence. Sensual accessories like bold purses, stiletto heels, and statement jewelry might go well with your look.

## 7.2 Embracing Self-Assurance

### 7.2.1 Body Confidence

Sensual sophistication is loving and appreciating your body. Honor your blemishes, scars, and curves as essential components of your sensuality.

### 7.2.2 Inexpressible Confidence

Try to project a sense of assurance and self-worth. To project sensuality, embrace eye contact, keep a straight spine, and move gracefully.

### 7.2.3 Hair and Makeup

Choose makeup that draws attention to your best features, such as smokey eyes, strong lips, or a dewy shine. Your seductive allure can also be enhanced by hairstyles that frame your face and emphasize your greatest features.

**7.2.4 Moderation and Balance**

Strike a balance between revealing too much and leaving enough to the imagination while embracing sexuality. The subtlety and allure of sensuous sophistication are its key components.

# 8. Honoring Cultural Attire by Adorning Traditional Beauty

Honoring cultural dress is a lovely way to honor your ancestry and celebrate your heritage. It's a fashion that cuts over national boundaries and enables you to showcase your individuality via

42

the extensive collection of heirloom items of clothing and jewelry.

## 8.1 Cultural Clothes and Accessories

### 8.1.1 Costumes of the Past

Add traditional attire from your area of origin to your wardrobe. Sarees, kimonos, cheongsams, and dashikis are more than just articles of apparel; they are representations of culture and identity.

### 8.1.2 Custom-made Accessories

Select handcrafted items that are influenced by your ethnic history, such as jewelry, scarves, or headpieces. These accessories give your outfit depth and authenticity.

### 8.1.3 Textiles and Embroidery

Investigate clothing and textiles that have elaborate embroidery, beadwork, or motifs that showcase your culture's artistry.

### 8.1.4 Modern Interpretations

For a contemporary spin, mix traditional pieces with contemporary components. For a fusion of styles, use a traditional blouse with jeans or a cultural skirt with a modern top.

## 8.2 Cultural Festival

### 8.2.1 Self-esteem and Pride

It is a sign of pride and a celebration of your identity to dress in cultural clothes. It's a method to respect your ancestry and maintain a relationship with it.

### 8.2.2 Fashion as a medium for storytelling

Every item of traditional clothing has a backstory and a purpose. You become a storyteller by wearing traditional beauty and sharing your culture's history.

### 8.2.3 Cultural Events and Occasions

When attending cultural events, festivals, or family get-togethers, cultural dress has a special significance. It's a way to honor your community's traditions and take part in them.

### 8.2.4 Cross-Cultural Understanding

Cultural dress encourages appreciation and understanding of other cultures. It encourages communication and links between various cultures.

## 9. The Fusion of Cross-Cultural Couture for the Modern Woman

Fashion that embraces the synthesis of several cultural influences is known as cross-cultural couture. It's about pushing borders, fusing customs, and using clothing to reflect your global perspective.

## 9.1 Support Fusion

### 9.1.1 Combining and Contrasting

Bring together components from several civilizations to produce a one-of-a-kind ensemble. Wear traditional designs with modern cuts, or pair a kimono-inspired jacket with a bohemian dress.

### 9.1.2 International Accessory

To add a multicultural flavor to your outfit, use accessories from many cultures, such as tribal-inspired jewelry, embroidered totes, or beaded shoes.

### 9.1.3 Cultural Colors and Patterns

Play around with hues and designs that have cultural resonance. To achieve a harmonious mix, use vivid colors, intricate prints, and geometric shapes.

### 9.1.4 Exploration of Textiles

Investigate textiles and fabrics from various countries. Silk and denim, batik and lace, or ikat and leather can all be combined to create a textural and eye-catching fusion.

## 9.2 Expression of Culture

### 9.2.1 Diversity of Identity

Your multicultural identity is celebrated through cross-cultural fashion. It's evidence of the many different factors that have molded your worldview.

### 9.2.2 Expression of the Arts

You can exhibit your originality and aesthetic sensibility through fusion fashion. You turn into a canvas on which various cultures mingle and clash.

### 9.2.3 International Dialogue

Talk starts and cultural interchange are promoted by wearing cross-cultural fashion. It's a chance to exchange tales and discover various customs.

### 9.2.4 Crossing Disparities

Cross-cultural fashion has the ability to heal rifts and promote harmony. It highlights the underlying similarities that bind us all together while celebrating variety.

Throughout this book we have traveled across the worlds of sensuous sophistication, cultural legacy, and cross-cultural fusion. Each of these fashions presents a different angle on self-expression, enabling you to embrace a global identity, celebrate your sexuality, and pay respect to your heritage. Remember that fashion is a canvas on which you paint your story, your beliefs, and your aspirations as you investigate and experiment with these styles. Your personal sense of fashion is a powerful expression of the world you live in and the woman you are growing into. We'll keep exploring different aspects of fashion expertise as we lead you to a better comprehension of your style potential.

# Part III: How to Dress for Every Situation

# 10. Day-to-Day Chic: Adding Style to Your Casual Clothes

The key to everyday stylish is adding flair and style to your casual attire. With this appearance, you may seem put together when going about your daily business, seeing friends for coffee, or taking a leisurely stroll around the park. It elevates your regular outfits.

## 10.1 The Heart of Everyday Chic

### 10.1.1 Laid-Back Elegance

Comfort and sophistication are balanced in everyday chic. It's about embracing unstructured silhouettes and cozy materials while incorporating refined details.

### 10.1.2 Easy-to-Apply Layers

Achieving everyday stylish requires layering. For a trendy yet relaxed look, combine essentials like t-shirts, lightweight sweaters, and cardigans.

### 10.1.3 Advanced Foundations

Spend money on top-notch foundational pieces for your casual outfit. Fitted jeans, adaptable shoes, and basic T-shirts are necessities.

### 10.1.4 Multipurpose Accessories

Casual clothing can be greatly improved with the right accessories. Make a fashion statement with bold sunglasses, a chic hat, or a crossbody bag.

## 10.2 Getting Everyday Chic

### 10.2.1 Comfortable jackets and blazers

To instantly boost your look, add a casual blazer or a thin jacket to your ensemble. It adds structure and gloss and is a flexible layering piece.

### 10.2.2 Fashionable flats and sneakers

Choose flats and sneakers that are both comfortable and stylish. Pick streamlined, elegant styles that you may wear with dresses, skirts, or pants.

### 10.2.3 Simple Makeup and Hairstyles

Accept easy-to-do but stylish hairstyles like untidy buns, beachy waves, or a straightforward ponytail. Choose a bright, natural makeup look.

### 10.2.4 Amusing Add-Ons

Accessories like striking earrings, stackable bracelets, or a vibrant scarf can provide a whimsical touch. A simple dress can become elegant with the addition of these accents.

# 11. Glamorous Evenings: Dressing to Dazzle

Elegant evenings provide a chance to shine and project refinement. The ability to command attention and make an impression lasts is made possible by mastering the art of dressing for beautiful evenings, whether you're attending a cocktail party, a formal dinner, or a special event.

## 11.1 The Glamorous Wardrobe

### 11.1.1 Dresses and Evening Gowns

Spend money on gorgeous evening dresses or gowns that fit your body and showcase your sense of style. Select looks that fit the situation and give you confidence.

### 11.1.2 Elegant Materials and Accents

For a hint of grandeur, choose opulent textiles like silk, satin, chiffon, or velvet. A dazzling glitter is added by embellishments like sequins, beading, or embroidery.

### 11.1.3 Statement-making Accessories

Make a fashion statement with your choice of accessories. Your look can be improved with a bold necklace, chandelier earrings, and a sparkling clutch.

### 11.1.4 Eye-catching Shoes

For a glamorous evening, you need footwear that matches your attire well. Excellent options include strappy sandals, heels with embellishments, and exquisite pumps.

## 11.2 Achieving Glamorous Perfection

### 11.2.1 Perfect hair and cosmetics

Spend some time crafting a beautiful and sophisticated hairdo. Choose stylish updos, thick curls, or Hollywood waves. To add drama to your makeup, go for strong lips or smoky eyes.

### 11.2.2 Pose and assurance

Glamour is more than simply what you wear; it's also how you carry yourself. To command the attention of the group, stand tall, move with assurance, and exude poise.

### 11.2.3 Posing Fit for a Red Carpet

Learn a few posing techniques to make the most of your attire. Try various stances, perspectives, and facial expressions to capture the glamour's essence.

### 11.2.4 Affectionate Presence

Engage with those around you and embrace the art of communication. Your charisma and presence are just as crucial to projecting a glamorous image as your outfit.

Keep in mind that each event presents a chance to show a different aspect of your personality as you explore the world of fashion and try out these looks. While you can embrace luxury and allure during dazzling evenings, day-to-day chic celebrates your easy charm. Both fashion choices demonstrate your versatility and elegance in any situation. You transform into a canvas with each piece of clothing, allowing you to express your self-assurance, sophistication, and unique style. As you continue to develop your understanding of various looks, you'll open up new doors to a world in which fashion is more than just a means of expression for apparel.

# 12. Wonders of the Wedding: Choosing the Ideal Guest Attire

Weddings are happy events full of excitement, celebration, and the chance to show off your personal flair as a guest. It's important to carefully evaluate the wedding theme, location, and dress code while choosing the ideal guest wear to strike the correct balance between formality, decorum, and individual style.

## 12.1 Understanding wedding attire guidelines

### 12.1.1 Formal and Black Tie

Choose sophisticated cocktail dresses or exquisite floor-length gowns for black-tie or formal weddings. For a timeless and sophisticated design, think about using traditional hues like black, navy, or deep jewel tones.

### 12.1.2 Cocktail and Semi-Formal Dress

Knee-length or midi dresses in vivid colors or amusing motifs are appropriate for semi-formal weddings. You may show off your personal flair in cocktail clothing by wearing stylish separates and knee-length dresses.

### 12.1.3 Beach and destination weddings

For beach or destination weddings, go for airy materials, flowing forms, and brilliant colors that go well with the laid-back atmosphere.

### 12.1.4 Outdoor and Garden Weddings

Weddings held in gardens or outdoors are ideal occasions for flowery designs, pastel hues, and breathable materials. Choose outfits that are both fashionable and cozy.

## 12.2 Appropriate Guest Attire

### 12.2.1 Honoring the Couple's Requests

When choosing your guest's outfit, always keep the couple's preferences and dress code in mind. Respect their requests if they specify a certain theme or color scheme.

### 12.2.2 Steer clear of white and ivory

Wearing these colors can take away from the bride's particular occasion, so save them for her. Choose a colorful outfit that shows your unique sense of flair.

### 12.2.3 Modesty and decorum

Choose attire that reflects the formality of the occasion and is respectful. Avoid wearing clothing that is too exposing or that might not fit the sacred nature of the ceremony.

### 12.2.4 Adaptable Shoes

Make sure your footwear is at ease so you may dance and revel all day or all night. Think of wearing embellished flats or chic block heels.

## 13. Cocktail Attire: How to Dress Perfectly and Fabulously

The ideal setting to show off your fashion-forward tastes while maintaining a polished and stylish appearance is a cocktail party. Choosing appropriate cocktail clothes can let you shine with effortless elegance at any cocktail party, networking event, or social gathering.

### 13.1 Cocktail Attire's Flexibility

#### 13.1.1 Elegant clothing

Select dresses that are flattering and acceptable length, hitting slightly above or below the knee. Pick exquisite fabrics and streamlined shapes.

### 13.1.2 Stylish Jumpsuits

Jumpsuits are becoming a mainstay of cocktail costumes, providing a chic and contemporary alternative to formal dresses. Choose jumpsuits with precise cuts and attention-grabbing accents.

### 13.1.3 Tailored Separates

Try wearing a fitting jacket with thin pants or a high-waisted skirt as a tailored separate. This adaptable strategy enables innovative pairings.

### 13.1.4 Fashionable Add-Ons

Add chic accessories to your cocktail attire to make it better. Glamour is added with statement jewelry, a clutch, and stiletto shoes.

## 13.2 Making a Statement

### 13.2.1 Vibrant hues and designs

Experimenting with bright colors and eye-catching patterns is encouraged when dressing for cocktails. By selecting colors with personality or fun prints, you may express yourself.

### 13.2.2 Contemporary Necklines

Investigate modern necklines such as asymmetrical, halter, or one-shoulder designs. These particulars give traditional cocktail wear a contemporary spin.

### 13.2.3 Texture and Embellishments

Use ornate accents, sequins, or textured fabrics to give your clothing depth. These components reflect light and arouse interest in the eye.

## 13.2.4 Smiling Face Makeup

Choose an elegant and self-assured hairdo like a classic blowout, tousled waves, or sleek updos. Make dramatic cosmetic choices that accentuate your inherent beauty to play up your attributes.

You unlock the door to a world of celebration and elegance as you enter the world of wedding wonders and cocktail wear. Wedding guest costume lets you show off your personal style while celebrating the happy couple's special day, while cocktail attire gives you the freedom to look chic in a range of social contexts. Your choice of clothing speaks volumes about your regard for tradition, your willingness to work within various dress rules, and your ability to convey your individual charm with style. Keep in mind that your presence is a gift and that the way you dress reflects the elegance and delight you bring to every situation.

## 14. A Walk Down the Aisle: Bridal Elegance and Beyond

The world of bridal elegance is one of magic, dreams, and the celebration of enduring love. On your wedding day, as the bride, you have the honor of personifying love, beauty, and joy. Bridal elegance goes beyond the wedding dress and includes everything you wear, including your accessories and makeup. It's an exploration of who you are, a reflection of your love story, and a voyage of painstaking planning.

## 14.1 The Wedding Group

### 14.1.1 The Ideal Wedding Dress

Selecting the ideal wedding dress is a profoundly intimate and transforming event. Think of silhouettes, materials, and finishing touches that complement your personal style and make you feel beautiful.

### 14.1.2 Headdresses, veils, and tiaras

Use veils, tiaras, or other headpieces that improve your overall aesthetic to accessorize your bridal appearance. These items provide a touch of tradition and ethereal elegance.

### 14.1.3 Jewelry and Accessorize

Choose jewelry that goes with your outfit and personal taste. You can infuse your outfit with sentimental value by adding delicate pearls, brilliant diamonds, or nostalgic accessories.

### 14.1.4 Bride-worthy footwear

Select stylish and comfy bridal shoes. Whether you choose elegant flats, classy heels, or edgy sandals, your shoes should express your style.

## 14.2 Grace and Beauty

### 14.2.1 Stylish Wedding Makeup

Your inherent beauty should be enhanced by bridal makeup, which should also keep you looking immaculate all day. To achieve ageless elegance, soft, neutral hues, and a luminous radiance are essential.

### 14.2.2 Accessorizing and Hair Styling

The style of your hair should go well with your outfit and facial features. Whether you choose a sophisticated updo, free-flowing waves, or a timeless bun, think about including hair accessories that improve your bridal look.

### 14.2.3 Details and Nail Art

Pay close care to your nails because they will be the center of attention when you display your wedding ring. Choose subtle, elegant nail art that enhances your entire style.

### 14.2.4 The Scent of Love

Pick a scent that perfectly expresses the spirit of your love story. The smell you wore on your wedding day will always bring back wonderful memories for you.

## 14.3 Dress for a Honeymoon Outside the Aisle

If you want to go from newlywed to honeymooner, you need to change your outfit. Pack functional clothing that will enable you to explore, unwind, and enjoy your honeymoon location.

### 14.3.1 Beachwear and Resort Clothing

Pack light resort clothes, swimsuits, and cover-ups that radiate effortless style if your honeymoon incorporates sandy beaches and turquoise oceans.

### 14.3.2 Dress for City Exploration

Choose attractive clothing, practical yet fashionable shoes, and accessories that let you take in the city's dynamic culture when traveling to urban areas.

### 14.3.3 Exploration and Adventure

If your honeymoon involves outdoor activities, bring sportswear, cozy shoes, and adaptable apparel so you may enjoy your experiences to the fullest.

### 14.3.4 Undies and Intimate Situations

Bring underwear that celebrates your new life together as a married couple. Select clothing that gives you a confident and alluring feeling.

Remember that your wedding day is the pinnacle of your love story as you set out on the journey of bridal elegance and beyond. This is an occasion to appreciate, celebrate, and embrace wholeheartedly. Your wedding attire serves as a blank canvas on which you can depict the romance, fashion, and dreams that are most important to you. Your honeymoon outfit becomes a reflection of the happiness, adventure, and shared experiences that you will have after you step down the aisle and into married life. You create a tapestry of elegance, beauty, and treasured memories that will always be a part of your love story with each decision you make, from the wedding dress to the perfume you wear.

# Part IV: Dressing Through the Seasons

## 15. Effortless Style for Blooming Days: Spring Splendor

Spring is a time of rebirth, growth, and the expectation of warmer weather. Your wardrobe beckons you to enjoy the vivacity and freshness of the season as the natural world awakens. Using brilliant colors, airy fabrics, and a joyful attitude to express the spirit of the blossoming days is how you wear spring splendor.

## 15.1 Embracing floral delights

### 15.1.1 Floral patterns and prints

Floral designs are a mainstay of spring magnificence because spring and florals go hand in hand. To create a vivid and feminine appearance, embrace delicate blossoms, strong florals, or abstract interpretations.

### 15.1.2 Floral Accents

Use accessories like scarves, headbands, or statement jewelry to add floral highlights. These accents give your outfit a hint of springtime charm.

### 15.1.3 A Fragrance With Flowers

With a scent that captures the spirit of blooming flowers, complete your spring wardrobe. Floral scents give your wardrobe a sensory dimension and express the mood of the season.

### 15.1.4 Pale and Vibrant Colors

Try out a color scheme of pastel tones and vibrant hues that mimics the range of hues present in springtime landscapes. Combine different elements for a fun and happy appearance.

## 15.2 Airy materials and simple layers

### 15.2.1 Fluffy Materials

Choose breathable, light fabrics like chiffon, linen, and cotton. You may enjoy the changing weather while remaining cozy with these fabrics.

### 15.2.2 Adding layers with jackets and cardigans

Because spring is a transitional season, layering is essential. To be fashionable and toasty, wear cardigans, denim jackets, or light blazers with your clothes.

**15.2.3 Fashionable Outerwear**

Pick elegant outerwear like trench coats, raincoats, or duster jackets. These accessories give a sense of refinement while shielding you from sudden showers.

**15.2.4 Amusing Accents**

The beauty of spring encourages you to experiment with seasonal accessories. For a stylish touch, think about using bright scarves, hats with wide brims, or woven purses.

# 16. Embracing Heat with Grace in the Summer

The essence of summer sizzle is to embrace the sun's warmth and shine while still exuding style and coziness. Your summer wardrobe embodies an effortless style that reflects the essence of the season, from breezy dresses to elegant swimwear.

## 16.1 Sun-Drenched Fashions

### 16.1.1 Maxi and midriff-baring dresses

Dresses with a maxi or midi length are classic summer items that are both comfortable and fashionable. Select breathable fabrics that let you move freely in the summertime heat.

### 16.1.2 Rompers and Sundresses

For carefree summer days, fun alternatives include sundresses and rompers. Choose eye-catching patterns, strong hues, or tropical designs to embody the carefree mood of the season.

### 16.1.3 Inconspicuous Jumpsuits

For the summer, jumpsuits provide a trendy and adaptable option. They seamlessly change from day to night, whether they are in solid colors or patterns.

### 16.1.4 Elegant Beachwear

Invest in fashionable swimwear that stands out. Whether it's a timeless one-piece or a chic bikini, pick swimsuits that complement your body shape and express your sense of style.

## 16.2 Maintaining Your Cool and Style

### 16.2.1 Shoes That Breathe

Choose breathable shoes that will keep your feet cool and comfy in the summer, such as espadrilles, strappy sandals, or slip-on sneakers.

### 16.2.2 Hats with Wide Brims

Wide-brimmed hats are a chic way to block the sun's rays. These add-ons provide both necessary sun protection and a dash of glitz.

### 16.2.3 Compact Cover-Ups

Use thin cover-ups like sheer wraps, sarongs, or kimonos to layer over your summer attire. These accessories provide adaptability and heat protection.

### 16.2.4 Statement sunglasses

Statement sunglasses that protect your eyes from the sun and give your outfit a bit of Hollywood glitz will finish off your summer wardrobe.

Your clothing transforms into a reflection of nature's beauty and the passing of time as you navigate the different seasons. While summer sizzle urges you to enjoy the warmth of the sun with grace and style, spring brilliance begs you to embrace the charm of blooming flowers and brilliant hues. Every season offers a chance to show off your individuality, adjust to the climate, and rejoice in the pleasures brought on by the changing scenery. Your clothes become a visual narrative of your relationship to the world around you, a monument to your ability to embrace the enchantment of every season with easy elegance, whether you're wearing floral designs in the spring sun or enjoying the appeal of summer chic.

# 17. The Allure of Autumn: Stunning Fall Fashion

The beauty of change is celebrated in the symphony of hues, textures, and layers that make up autumn's attraction. Your outfit changes at the same time that the leaves change and the air becomes crisper. This season asks you to embrace warm hues, adaptable outfits, and soft fabrics that perfectly express the allure of fall.

## 17.1 Accepting Autumnal Colors

### 17.1.1 Jewel tones and earthy tones

Take advantage of the cozy and inviting fall color palette, which features rich jewel tones like burgundy and emerald alongside earthy tones like rust, olive, and mustard.

### 17.1.2 Patterns in Plaid and Checks

Dress for fall by using classic plaid and check patterns. These designs offer a touch of refinement to everything from soft scarves to sharp blazers.

### 17.1.3 Switching Between Neutrals

Neutral colors like taupe, camel, and gray are important to incorporate as we move from summer to fall. Your autumnal outfits are built on these adaptable hues.

### 17.1.4 Metallic Accents

Metallic touches will give your fall clothes a dash of glitz. Details made of gold, bronze, and copper create an air of wealth and richness.

## 17.2 Layers and Textures

### 17.2.1 Cozy sweaters and knits

Spend money on warm, fashionable knits and sweaters. For a stylish appearance, use thick cable knits, large cardigans, and turtleneck sweaters.

### 17.2.2 Fashionable Coats

Fall is the ideal season to display fashionable outerwear, such as quilted jackets, trench coats, and fitted coats. Your ensembles will be more structured and elegant with these elements.

### 17.2.3 Scarves for Layering

With scarves in a variety of textures and patterns, you may wrap yourself in flair. Your autumnal outfit can be improved with infinity scarves, blanket scarves, and silk scarves.

### 17.2.4 Booties and ankle boots

Fall footwear must include booties and ankle boots. They can be worn with skirts, dresses, or jeans for a varied and fashionable style.

# 18. Cozy Clothing for Cold Days from Winter Wonders

The majesty of a snow-covered landscape, a warm gathering, and the joy of a holiday celebration are all captured in winter wonders. Your winter wardrobe transforms into a blank canvas for showcasing your personal style while remaining warm and cozy in chilly weather.

## 18.1 Adopting Winter Textiles

### 18.1.1 Wool and cashmere

Choose clothing made of wool and cashmere for their insulation and suppleness. These fabrics make cozy and toasty sweaters, scarves, and coats.

### 18.1.2 Shearling and Faux Fur

For a hint of luxury, add faux fur and shearling accents. Your winter ensembles get cozier and more elegant thanks to these textures.

### 18.1.3 Elegant Velvet

Investigate the depth of velvet, a material that oozes class and sophistication. Dresses, skirts, and accessories made of velvet give your look a regal vibe.

### 18.1.4 Thermal Layers

Winter requires a lot of layering, and thermal underwear adds a layer of warmth without adding bulk. These items are necessary for maintaining comfort.

## 18.2 Winter Equipment

### 18.2.1 Fashionable Beanies and Berets

Wear trendy beanies and berets to be warm and fashionable. These items keep you warm and give your winter attire a whimsical twist.

### 18.2.2 Statement mittens and gloves

Use useful and fashionable statement gloves or mittens as an accessory. To draw attention, go for strong hues, patterns, or embellishments.

### 18.2.3 comfier scarves and wraps

Keep the cold at bay by wrapping up warm scarves and blankets. The stylistic possibilities are endless with blanket scarves, infinity scarves, and large wraps.

### 18.2.4 Footwear Fit for Winter

Pick winter-appropriate footwear like insulated booties, knee-high boots, or snow boots. These choices offer warmth and defense against snow and ice.

While the chilly winter weather tempts you to embrace warmth and comfort with opulent textures and layers, the fascinating colors and textures of autumn inspire you to explore a rich palette of earthy tones and comforting textiles. Your ability to find beauty and elegance in every moment, whether it be a walk through fallen leaves or a chilly night by the fireplace, is reflected in how you construct a visual story with each season. Your fashion sense changes with the seasons, showcasing your versatile and dynamic approach to style that adapts to all environments and thrives there.

# Part V: Dressing with Confidence

# 19. The Confidence Effect: Your Empowerment via Clothes

The relationship between appearance and self-assurance is a potent combination that can change how you see yourself and how other people see you. Beyond only looks, the confidence effect is a psychological phenomenon that affects your attitude, actions, and interactions. You may tap into an inner source of confidence when you dress with purpose and wear clothes that complement your particular style.

## 19.1 The Psychology of Clothing

### 19.1.1 The Halo Effect

The halo effect is a cognitive bias in which favorable traits connected to one part of a person's personality affect how we view those other characteristics. The halo effect, which improves how people view your intelligence, competence, and social skills, can be brought on by dressing well.

### 19.1.2 Clad Cognitive Processes

The concept of enclothed cognition holds that your clothing has an impact on your thoughts and actions. Wearing attire that inspires confidence, achievement, or happy memories might improve performance and foster a more upbeat attitude.

### 19.1.3 Self-Fulfilling Prophecy

The way you present yourself can influence how you interact and how things turn out. Positive encounters and accomplishments are more likely to occur if you feel you present a confident, polished image.

## 19.2 Style as Empowerment

### 19.2.1 Attire for the Situation

You may feel in control and ready to face the issue if you dress appropriately. You're more likely to address issues with poise and confidence when you're dressed appropriately.

### 19.2.2 Putting Yourself Out There

You can show your personality, ideals, and creativity via the clothes you wear. Embracing distinctive looks and striking pieces enables you to stand out and show off your authenticity.

### 19.2.3 Mood-Boosting

Your mood and spirit can be improved by your clothing. Wearing your favorite clothes or brightly colored accessories can instantly uplift your mood and make your day more enjoyable.

### 19.2.4 Strength of the Channel

Strong and empowering sensations might be evoked by particular clothing items or fashion trends. Choose outfits that make you feel strong and capable to embrace power dressing.

# 20. Promoting body positivity by embracing each curve

Body positivity is a movement that places a strong emphasis on loving and accepting oneself and enjoying the diversity of all body types. You may dress with confidence, appreciate your individual beauty, and express yourself honestly by embracing body positivity.

## 20.1 Accepting Self-Love

### 20.1.1 Rejecting Unrealistic Standards

By rejecting unreasonable expectations and embracing your natural body form, you can subvert socially acceptable notions of beauty. Celebrate the individuality and natural beauty of your body.

### 20.1.2 Finding Balance

Find a happy medium between good health and self-acceptance. Recognizing that beauty comes in numerous ways, concentrate on feeling well both physically and mentally.

### 20.1.3 Mindful Mirror Reflections

When staring in the mirror, use mindfulness and encouraging language. Think about the aspects of your body that you love and be grateful for the adventure it has provided for you.

### 20.1.4 How to Dress for Your Individual Body

Choose outfits that highlight your best qualities and give you a relaxed, confident feeling. Adopt clothing that reflects your uniqueness and gives you a sense of empowerment.

## 20.2 Using clothing to express oneself

### 20.2.1 Curating a Confidence Wardrobe

Create a wardrobe that complements your physical features and personal taste. Select clothing that reflects your unique style and gives you a sense of confidence.

### 20.2.2 Trying Different Styles

Experiment with diverse styles, silhouettes, and colors outside of your comfort zone. Accept fashion as a fun and inventive means of expression.

### 20.2.3 Making Courageous Decisions

Encourage yourself to make audacious decisions. Allow yourself to confidently enter the spotlight by wearing a statement piece, baring flesh, or experimenting with a new trend.

### 20.2.4 Motivating Other People

Set an example for others and promote body positivity. Celebrate individuality, provide praise, and promote an atmosphere of encouragement and self-acceptance.

You start a transformational journey that includes both internal and outward empowerment as you explore the worlds of confidence and body positivity. The confidence effect serves as a reminder of the tremendous impact that clothing has on how you feel about yourself and how you come across to others. You can use clothing as a weapon for self-assurance and success by matching your appearance to your aspirations and adopting empowering fashions. Parallel to this, body positivity exhorts you to see your body as a blank canvas that may be painted with beauty, strength, and authenticity. It's a movement that goes beyond fashion trends and encourages you to love and accept yourself. You develop into a champion for empowerment, self-expression, and the celebration of every curve that makes you uniquely you as you traverse the nexus of confidence and body acceptance.

## 21. The Magic of Accessories: Adding Elegance to Any Look

Even the most basic of clothes may achieve new levels of elegance and style thanks to the transformational power of accessories. Your outfit's full potential can be unlocked by adding these understated yet significant finishing touches, which will let you express your personality, improve your appearance, and leave a lasting impression.

### 21.1 Statement Jewelry

#### 21.1.1 Pendants and Necklaces

A statement necklace can take center stage in any outfit, emphasizing your neckline and adding a touch of glitz.

### 21.1.2 Ear cuffs and jewelry

Earrings can be utilized to frame your face, brighten your outfit, or give it a contemporary edge. A stylish and distinctive way to accessorize your ears is with ear cuffs.

### 21.1.3 Bracelets and Bangles

Your wrists are adorned with bracelets and bangles, which offer a touch of style and motion. Combine and contrast several styles for a unique result.

### 21.1.4 Rings and stackable bands

To show off your distinct style, stack or wear individual rings. Play around with various metals, gems, and designs.

## 21.2 Multipurpose Shawls & Scarves

### 21.2.1 Silk Scarves

Silk scarves are highly adaptable and can be used as handbag accents, neckties, or headbands. They provide your clothing with a splash of color and texture.

### 21..2.2 Cozy blankets and scarves

Warmth and sophistication come together with blanket scarves, which you can wear around your neck or drape over your shoulders for a stylish layered effect.

### 21.2.3 Elegant Shawls

Shawls add a sophisticated touch to evening attire. For a chic and elegant look, wrap them around your shoulders.

## 21.3 Belts for Definition

### 21.3.1 Tighten Your Belt

Belts can help you accentuate your waist and give flowy clothing some rigidity. From thin and delicate to large and bold, they are available in a variety of sizes and designs.

### 21.3.2 Coats and dresses with belts

Add a belt to dresses and coats to give them a more streamlined and refined silhouette. This method can improve comfort and style.

### 21.3.3 Tassel belts for a Bohemian look

Your ensembles will have a bohemian feel thanks to tassel belts. Put them on to give a fun and whimsical touch to dresses, tunics, or high-waisted jeans.

## 21.4 Fashionable Purses & Bags

### 21.4.1 Chic Everyday Tote Bags

Tote bags are useful and fashionable, providing lots of room for your necessities while also enhancing your look with their style.

### 21.4.2 Crossbody Bags with On-the-Go Style

Hands-free carrying and convenience are made possible with crossbody bags. They are perfect for going on errands or having a fashionable city tour.

### 21.4.3 Elegant Evening Clutches

Add refinement and a dash of glitz to your ensemble with a beautiful clutch to elevate your evening wear.

# 22. Sustainable Fashion: Making Sense of the Industry

Fashion that respects the environment, labor rights, and social responsibility are embraced by sustainable style, which stands for a commitment to moral and environmentally friendly fashion choices. You can contribute to a more just and sustainable fashion business while also expressing your ideals via your clothing by navigating the industry with a conscience.

## 22.1 Sustainability's Vitality

### 22.1.1 Environmental Impact

Learn about the effects of fast fashion on the environment and the advantages of using sustainable resources and manufacturing techniques.

### 22.1.2 Moral Business Conduct

Recognize the importance of reasonable pay, a safe work environment, and the welfare of garment workers in the fashion sector.

### 22.1.3 Waste Reduction

Investigate strategies for reducing clothing waste, such as recycling, reusing, and taking part in clothes exchanges.

### 22.1.4 The Sluggish Fashion Trend

Invest in high-quality, classic pieces that will last a lifetime to embrace the slow fashion movement.

## 22.2 Choices That Are Moral and Sustainable

### 22.2.1 Natural and organic textiles

Choose clothing produced from sustainable materials like organic cotton, hemp, bamboo, or other natural fibers.

### 22.2.2 Eco-friendly Dyes

Choose clothing that has been colored with environmentally and skin-friendly dyes that do the least amount of harm.

### 22.2.3 Buys from Estate Sales and Vintage Shops

Find secondhand items that lower the demand for new production by perusing thrift stores, vintage shops, and online marketplaces.

**22.2.4 Local and artisanal brands**

In order to boost the local economy and encourage sustainable practices, support regional designers and artisans.

# 23. Dressing for Different Body Types to Boost Confidence

You may celebrate your individuality, highlight your strengths, and enhance your proportions by dressing for your particular body type. You may create a wardrobe that enhances your figure and gives you more confidence if you are aware of the subtleties of various body shapes.

## 23.1 Accepting Body Diversity

### 23.1.1 Hourglass Figure

Fitted clothes and precise silhouettes will draw attention to your waist. Particularly attractive clothing includes A-line skirts and wrap dresses.

### 23.1.2 Shape of a pear

By emphasizing your upper body with statement shirts and emphasizing your shoulders with volume or detailing, you may balance your proportions.

### 23.1.3 An apple

Choose dresses with A-line skirts and empire waistlines to balance your appearance by detracting attention from your midsection.

### 23.1.4 Rectangular Figure

Peplum shirts, tight waistlines, and dresses that lend dimension to your form will help you create curves.

## 23.2 Style Advice to Inspire Confidence

### 23.2.1 Outfits in One Color

Your silhouette will be lengthened and have an appearance of sophistication thanks to monochromatic outfits that generate a vertical line.

### 23.2.2 Vertical Lines and Patterns

Vertical stripes and patterns increase the perception of space by drawing the eye higher and below.

### 23.2.3 Strategic Layering

Layering can improve the natural proportions of your body and give dimension. Try out different lengths and textures.

### 23.2.4 Tailoring's Power

Invest in fitted clothing or get your existing wardrobe modified for the best fit that complements your body type.

As you embrace sustainable fashion, the enchantment of accessorizing, and the skill of dressing for all body shapes, you set off on a journey of empowerment, consciousness, and self-expression. Your partners in upgrading each look, adding unique flair, and increasing the impact of your ensemble are your accessories. A commitment to ethical fashion choices that are good for the environment and you means that your wardrobe should reflect your principles. You also start along a path of self-acceptance as you celebrate the beauty and uniqueness of your form as you personalize your confidence by clothing for your particular body type. Every step you take along the way will help you develop a comprehensive view of fashion—one that empowers you, raises your soul and portrays the complex, conscious woman you are.

# Part VI: Beyond Clothing

# 24. The Art of Makeup: Enhancing Your Natural Beauty

You can emphasize your individual beauty, convey your mood, and improve your characteristics with the help of makeup, which is a creative and empowering tool. Beyond just being aesthetically pleasing, makeup is a kind of self-expression that encourages you to embrace your uniqueness and exude confidence.

## 24.1 The Fundamentals of Applying Makeup

### 24.1.1 Skincare as a Foundation

Make skincare a priority to create a flawless surface for applying makeup. Cleanse, hydrate, and use SPF to protect your skin.

### 24.1.2 Perfect Composure

Use setting powder, concealer, and foundation to achieve a flawless face. To achieve a natural look, pick colors that complement your skin tone.

### 24.1.3 Improving Your Vision

To define and emphasize your eyes, experiment with mascara, eyeliners, and eyeshadows. Natural styles, winged eyeliner, and smoky eyes are all adaptable choices.

### 24.1.4 Delicate Lips

Look into a variety of lip colors, from subtle to dramatic, to complete your appearance. Lipsticks, lip liners, and lip glosses give lips depth and color.

## 24.2 Accepting Your Individual Style

### 24.2.1 Day-to-Night Transition

Learn how to change your daytime makeup into a nighttime look by giving your features more drama, depth, and intensity.

### 24.2.2 Playing Around with Color

To reflect your personality and mood, experiment with color. You can express your creativity by using vibrant eyeshadows, bold lips, and original looks.

### 24.2.3 Natural and makeup-free looks

Learn how to look natural and fresh while highlighting your characteristics without being overdone.

### 24.2.4 Special Occasion Glamour

Makeup for special occasions can be elevated by using tricks like contouring, highlighting, and fake lashes.

# 25. Finding Your Signature Hairstyle with Hair Mastery

Your hair may be a dynamic canvas for personal style and expression. Finding your unique hairstyle enables you to appreciate the natural texture of your hair, try out various styles, and project confidence with each hair flip.

## 25.1 Accepting Your Hair Texture

### 25.1.1 Hair that is curly and oily

Utilize items that hydrate your curls and coils while enhancing their definition.

### 25.1.2 Straight hair

Try different polished and sleek haircuts to show off the beauty of your straight hair.

### 25.1.3 Wavy Hair

Texturizing hair treatments and funky haircuts that celebrate the carefree allure of wavy hair can enhance your waves.

### 25.1.4 Natural Hair

Discover updos, twists, and protective styles that highlight the beauty and adaptability of your natural hair.

## 25.2 Artistic Hairdos

### 25.2.1 Simple Upstyles

Learn how to create simple, stylish updos for both casual and formal settings. Top knots, chignons, and buns provide a polished appearance.

### 25.2.2 Elegant Curls

Using curling irons, rollers, or braiding methods, produce glam curls. Hairstyles with curls radiate a classic charm.

### 25.2.3 Elegant Ponies

Create variants on the traditional ponytail that are sleek and high-shine to elevate it. Ponytails are adaptable and work well in a variety of scenarios.

### 25.2.4 Braided Beauty

Try out different braiding techniques, such as elaborate fishtails, crown braids, and traditional three-strand braids.

Beyond clothing, makeup and hairstyles become crucial components in your path toward style. The skill of cosmetics improves your inherent beauty and enables you to try out many looks that reflect your mood and personality. You find a new avenue of self-expression and creativity that goes along with your sense of style as you experiment with cosmetics techniques.

Understanding different hairstyles gives you the capacity to show off your personality and mood because your hair is an aspect of your unique identity. Accept the natural texture of your hair, try out expressive looks, and compile a collection of go-to looks that reflect your distinctive hairstyle. Your capacity to create a complete and polished image of yourself—one that represents your confidence, style, and inner beauty—expands as you immerse yourself in the world of makeup and hair artistry.

# 26. The Power of Fragrance: The Style Statement of Perfume

An intangible item with the capacity to arouse strong feelings and leave a lasting impression is fragrance. The skill of choosing the ideal scent is a sophisticated technique to improve your own style, leaving an odorous impression on those you come into contact with.

## 26.1 The Perfume's Essence

### 26.1.1 Families of Fragrances

Learn about the various perfume families, such as floral, oriental, woody, and fresh scents. You can find scents that fit your style by understanding these categories.

### 26.1.2 Notes and Accords

From top to bottom, reveal the layers of the scent notes. A rich smell profile is produced by notes including citrus, flowery, and musk and changes over time.

### 26.1.3 Continuity and Sillage

Learn how to assess a perfume's sillage (how far the scent projects) and duration (how long it lasts on your skin). The ideal perfume can be chosen with the use of this expertise.

## 26.2 Application and Choice of Fragrances

### 26.2.1 Personal Relationship

Pick a scent that appeals to your personality and makes you feel good. Your style and unique personality should be reflected in your choice of fragrance.

### 26.2.2 Situation-Perfect Scents

Make your choice of perfume appropriate for each occasion. Choose milder scents during the day and stronger scents on evening occasions.

### 26.2.3 Layering and blending

Try mixing several fragrances to create a distinctive scent signature. Your olfactory style gains a personal touch when you mix scents.

### 26.2.4 Appropriate Use

Use pulse points when applying perfume for the best diffusion. The best places to enhance the fragrance's projection are the wrists, neck, and behind the ears.

# 27. Elevate with Aromas: Picking the Best Body Sprays, Deodorants, and Perfumes

Choosing the proper perfume is just the beginning of upping your scent game; you also need to add complimentary scents through body sprays and deodorants. This multi-layered strategy guarantees a seamless and robust olfactory experience.

## 27.1 Deodorants Offer More Than Just Odor Control

### 27.1.1 Deodorants with Scents

Look into scented deodorants that provide odor protection as well as a light aroma. For a consistent aroma, match the deodorant and perfume you intend to wear.

### 27.1.2 Formulas for deodorants

Depending on your requirements, choose between antiperspirant and deodorant formulations. Antiperspirants prevent sweating and provide a pleasant fragrance.

### 27.1.3 Options that are natural and free of aluminum

Think about deodorants that are natural and aluminum-free that have an emphasis on ingredient transparency and skin health.

## 27.2 Enhancing body sprays

### 27.2.1 Fresh and Light

Body sprays offer a revitalizing aroma burst that can be applied repeatedly throughout the day. They are perfect for a rapid mood boost.

### 27.2.2 Additional Aromas

Choose body sprays that go well with the perfume or deodorant you've chosen. The layered technique gives your smell profile depth and richness.

### 27.2.3 Convenience for On-the-Go

Body sprays enable you to keep up a constant odor throughout your everyday activities, making them ideal for touch-ups on-the-go.

You discover a completely new way to express your sense of style as you explore deeper into the world of perfumes. By enticing others around you with a scent that symbolizes your individuality and heightens your charm, perfume transforms into a seductive approach to leave a lasting impression of your presence. By carefully choosing body sprays, deodorants, and perfumes that complement your style, you heighten your sensory experience and further hone your capacity to make an individual statement.

# Part VII: Navigating Fashion Trends

# 28. Using High Fashion in Your Wardrobe: Decoding Runway Trends

You may add the newest runway-inspired styles to your wardrobe by navigating fashion trends, which is an exciting and dynamic trip. Understanding runway trends gives you the power to translate high fashion ideas to your own personal style, enabling you to put together looks that are current, distinctive, and true to your character.

## 28.1 Revealing runway trends

### 28.1.1 Fashion Weeks & Collections

Visit the world of fashion weeks to see how designers present their most recent works. Learn about forthcoming silhouettes and trends.

### 28.1.2 Trend analysis

Learn how to decipher the repeating themes, color schemes, fabrics, and details that characterize current fashion trends from runway displays.

### 28.1.3 Putting Runway into Practice

Know how to translate high fashion ideas into appropriate attire that complements your personal style and daily activities.

## 28.2 Adapting Runway Trends

### 28.2.1 Utilizing Statement Items

Choose one or two runway-inspired statement pieces and create an outfit around them. This method gives your ensemble a modern edge.

### 28.2.2 Mixing Trends

Try blending various trends to create a one-of-a-kind, customized look. Intriguing contrasts between elements are juxtaposed.

### 28.2.3 Using Accessory Infusion

To increase the fashionable look of your ensemble, add trend-inspired accessories like bags, shoes, and jewelry.

### 28.2.4 Exploration of Color

Play around with fresh color schemes and combinations that are influenced by runway trends. Your wardrobe will be revitalized with these vibrant new colors.

## 29. Vintage Revival: Integrating Classic Pieces into Contemporary Looks

The attractiveness of vintage clothing is in its capacity to withstand the test of time, providing a chance to add classic elegance and personality to your current wardrobe. By embracing vintage revival, you may pay homage to the past while designing modern costumes that draw inspiration from the long history of fashion.

## 29.1 Vintage Allure

### 29.1.1 Examining Various Epochs

Explore vintage fashion from the glitzy 1920s through the free-spirited 1970s. Learn about the unique fashions from each era.

### 29.1.2 Timeless silhouettes

Recognize classic silhouettes that still hold the attention of the fashion industry, such as pencil skirts, A-line dresses, and high-waisted pants.

### 29.1.3 Original Creations

Appreciate the distinctive textiles and fabrics that characterized many eras, from opulent silk and lace to useful denim and wool.

## 29.2 Adding Vintage to Modern Styles

### 29.2.1 Combination

To create a balanced and appealing ensemble, combine vintage and modern pieces. Depth is added by the contrast of the ancient and new.

### 29.2.2 Statement Equipment

Add a touch of nostalgia to your contemporary clothes with vintage accessories like hats, scarves, and brooches.

### 29.2.3 Tailoring for Today

Modify old clothing to fit your body and your sense of style. Custom tailoring guarantees that your vintage clothing fits invisibly with the rest of your wardrobe.

### 29.2.4 Vintage-inspired Styling

To finish your retro-modern appearance, use vintage-inspired styling techniques like pin curls, victory rolls, or cat-eye eyeliner.

## 29.3 Eco-Friendly Clothing

### 29.3.1 Environmental Impact

The use of old clothing reduces the need for new production and cuts down on clothing waste, both of which are beneficial to sustainable fashion.

### 29.3.2 Telling Personal Stories

Each antique item has a distinct history and narrative. You can create your own fashion narrative by incorporating old pieces into your contemporary collection.

### 29.3.3 Ethical Consumerism

By recycling and reusing clothing, patronizing vintage and thrift stores encourages ethical consumption and lessens the environmental impact of the fashion industry.

Incorporating runway inspiration into your own wardrobe, you embrace the ebb and flow of style evolution as you navigate fashion trends. Understanding high fashion concepts enables you to create ensembles that seamlessly combine modern and cutting-edge components, producing looks that are on-trend and totally you.

Contrarily, vintage revival invites you to resuscitate classic pieces and elegantly incorporate them into your contemporary outfits while transporting you back in time via the history of fashion. By paying homage to the past, you give old clothing new life, conserving its charm and helping to promote a sustainable and ethical attitude to fashion.

A seamless fusion of the avant-garde and the classic is produced by the examination of runway trends and the resurgence of vintage clothing. The result is a wardrobe that is adaptable, creative, and a real representation of your individuality. This dynamic synergy advances your style while paying attention to the rich tapestry of fashion's past.

## 30. Style Evolution: Adapting Your Wardrobe with Changing Trends

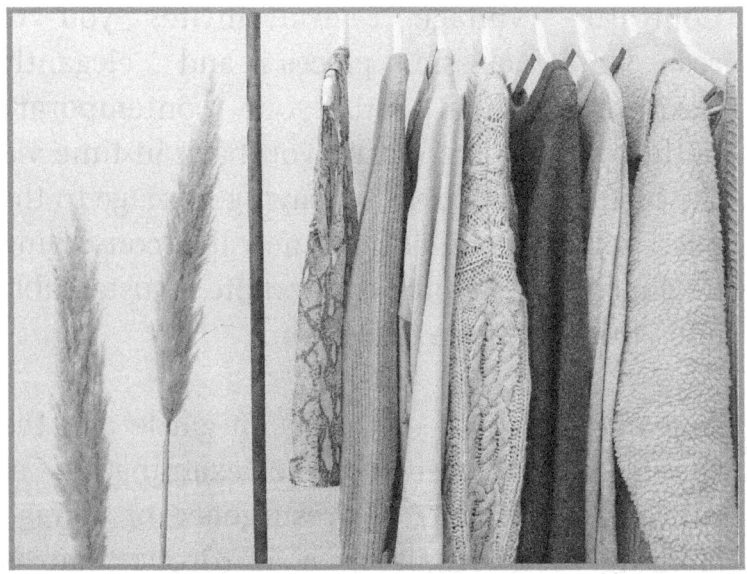

Personal style is a journey that always evolves, and adjusting your wardrobe to new trends is a crucial element of that evolution. Your capacity to adapt to these changes enables you to keep an up-to-date appearance that fits your personality and way of life as fashion trends continue to change and evolve.

## 30.1 The Evolution of Style: Its Nature

### 30.1.1 Adapting to Change

Recognize that fashion is dynamic and constantly evolving. Explore new trends with interest, and update your outfit to reflect them.

### 30.1.2 Ongoing Education

Through fashion periodicals, online resources, social media, and fashion events, keep up with the most recent fashion trends.

### 30.1.3 Reflecting on Personal Development

As you develop and alter as a person, let your style adapt along with you. Your fashion choices may reflect your goals and progress in life.

## 30.2 Transitional Clothing Essentials

### 30.2.1 Classical Works as Anchors

Make your changing style's base out of classic wardrobe essentials. As you experiment with trends, these pieces offer consistency.

### 30.2.2 Mixing the Old and New

Combine timeless pieces with trend-driven ones to put together a balanced and well-coordinated look that perfectly encapsulates the spirit of the season.

### 30.2.3 Creative Layering

By integrating various pieces and textures through layering, you may combine current trends with wardrobe staples.

## 30.3 Investigation and Experimentation

### 30.3.1 Attempting New Looks

Be open to experimenting with fashions that are unfamiliar to you. Making new fashion discoveries can be unexpected and thrilling by experimenting with trends.

### 30.3.2 Using Ideas from Various Epochs

To develop a distinctive and varied look that demonstrates your style evolution, draw inspiration from many fashion eras.

## 30.4 Evolution of Sustainable Style

30.4.1 Consuming awareness

Invest in high-quality items that will last and go with your growing style to practice mindful buying.

### 30.4.2 Upcycling and Repurposing

Utilize upcycling and repurposing techniques to turn worn-out objects into new, fashionable goods.

### 30.4.3 Wardrobes in Capsules

Think about building a capsule wardrobe with an emphasis on adaptable and classic pieces to make it simpler to keep up with fashion trends.

### 30.4.4 Vintage and ethical clothing

In order to lessen your impact on the environment and promote ethical purchasing, include sustainable and antique clothing in your personal style.

## 30.5 Adopting Your True Style

### 30.5.1 Trust in Change

With assurance and self-assurance, approach style evolution understanding that change is a necessary component of personal development.

### 30.5.2 Following Your Gut Feeling

Trust your wardrobe choices and pay attention to your gut. Your individual taste and personality are reflected in your changing sense of style.

### 30.5.3 Authentic Expression

Use your sense of style to express yourself. Accept the trends that speak to your inner self and let your personal style develop naturally.

You embrace the ever-evolving nature of fashion as you set off on the voyage of style evolution with poise and zeal. It becomes a creative and empowering process to modify your clothing in response to emerging trends because it enables you to constantly reinvent your appearance while being true to your genuine self. This development is a tribute to your fashion discovery, a celebration of your personal development, and a reminder that your style is an ever-evolving canvas that defines your identity.

# Part VIII Exploring the World of Accessories

Your clothing can be transformed into something extraordinary with the help of accessories. They have the ability to give your outfit depth, individuality, and flair, enabling you to convey your sense of style deftly and imaginatively. This part delves into the alluring world of accessories and teaches you how to choose, layer, and mix different items to create a look that is totally you.

## 31. How to Choose, Layer, and Mix Pieces of Jewelry

Jewelry is a classic and adaptable item that embodies style and originality. It has the amazing capacity to draw attention to your characteristics, capture your mood, and convey a narrative through its design. Learn how to choose, layer, and mix jewelry items to create eye-catching outfits that reflect your particular style.

### 31.1 Picking Out Jewelry

#### 31.1.1 Statement necklaces

Statement necklaces attract attention and make your look stand out. Select striking patterns that express your personality and work with your neckline.

### 31.1.2 Earrings for Every Occasion

Earrings come in a variety of styles, from chic chandeliers to subtle studs. For a coordinated look, match your earrings to your attire and the event.

### 31.1.3 Bracelets and Bangles

Your wrists are made more elegant and dynamic by bracelets and bangles. Play around with stacking various items to make a carefully chosen and unique arm party.

### 31.1.4 Rings: From Delicate to Dazzling

Rings stand for sentiment and style. Wear rings that have special importance or just to show off your sense of style and decoration.

## 31.2 Jewelry mixing and layering

### 31.2.1 Metal blending

Accept the skill of metal blending to provide a unique and modern appearance. Rose gold, silver, and combinations of these metals provide depth and visual intrigue.

### 31.2.2 Layered necklaces

Create a cascading effect by layering delicate necklaces of various lengths to highlight your neckline and give your ensemble more depth.

### 31.2.3 Rings that stack

For a fun and adaptable arrangement, stack rings of various shapes and sizes on one finger or across several fingers.

### 31.2.4 Pairing of Earrings

For an edgy and contemporary look, play around with asymmetrical earring combinations or combine studs and statement earrings.

# 32. Hats & Headwear: A Touch of Elegance

Hats and other headgear add an air of sophistication and mystery, taking your ensemble to new levels of elegance. They provide shade, warmth, and an eye-catching focal point for your attire, serving as both useful and stylistic elements.

## 32.1 Different Hat and Headwear Styles

Classic Wide-Brim Hats 32.1.1

Wide-brimmed hats radiate a classic elegance while shielding the sun. Put them in fitted pieces, dresses, or skirts.

### 32.1.2 Trendy Beanies

Berets give your ensemble a Parisian flair and go nicely with casual, bohemian, or even formal attire.

### 32.1.3 Headbands and other hair ornaments

Your hairdo is given a whimsical and feminine touch by headbands, hairpins, and ornamental combs, allowing you to try out different designs.

### 32.1.4 Fascinators and formal headgear

Consider elegant and charming fascinators, headpieces, or embellished hairpins for special events.

### 32.2 Hats and Headwear: How to Style

### 32.2.1 Coordinating Hats

Make sure your hat matches the color scheme and design of your outfit. Your complete look can be brought together with a well-chosen hat.

### 32.2.2 Casual and undemanding

For a carefree and effortlessly stylish style, team a wide-brim hat with a flowy dress, sandals, and striking sunglasses.

### 32.2.3 Accessorizing with Hats

When attending weddings, galas, or high-profile events, accessorize your formal clothes with elaborate headpieces or fascinators.

### 32.2.4 Accessorizing Your Hair for Everyday Glam

If you want to spice up your regular hairstyles, whether you're going to the workplace or meeting friends for brunch, use headbands, hairpins, and colorful combs.

## 33. Bags and Beyond: Finding the Ideal Handbag for Every Look

Handbags are both practical and expressive, acting as a chic storage solution for your necessities and expressing your personal style and way of life. Knowing how to choose the ideal purse for each outfit makes sure that your look is put together and fashionable.

### 33.1 Handbag Styles

#### 33.1.1 Tote bags

Totes are perfect for transporting your daily essentials or even your business essentials because they are roomy and multipurpose.

#### 33.1.2 Crossbody Bags

Crossbody bags are ideal for hectic days and city adventures since they provide convenience and hands-free mobility.

#### 33.1.3 Evening bags and clutches

For formal events, clutches and evening purses lend a touch of class. Select patterns that go well with your attire or robe.

## 33.1.4 Bags and Other Lightweight Carriers

For day trips, vacations, and urban exploration, backpacks are stylish and practical.

## 33.2 Coordinating Bags with Outfits

## 33.2.1 Coordination of Colors

To achieve a coordinated and put-together look, coordinate the color of your purse with the colors in your outfit.

## 33.2.2 Formal versus casual attire

Pick a purse design that complements the formality of your attire. crossbody bags for casual outings and clutches for formal occasions.

### 33.2.3 Statement handbags

With a distinctive or striking handbag that gives your look originality and flair, make a strong fashion statement.

### 33.2.4 Multipurpose Neutrals

Invest in neutral handbags in shades like black, brown, or nude so they can go with a number of outfits.

## 33.3 Beyond Handbags

### 33.3.1 Belts as Accessories

Belts are adaptable accessories that define your waist, cinch your waist, and boost your appearance. Try out various belt placements and styles.

### 33.3.2 Scarves are fashionable and practical.

Scarves can be used as belts, headbands, and accessories to give flair and warmth to any ensemble.

### 33.3.3 Statement eyewear

Sunglasses are necessary accessories that not only shield your eyes but also elevate your look.

### 33.3.4 Bracelets and watches

Your wrist will look more sophisticated with watches and bracelets, which can also be layered for a fashionable and textured look.

Accessories are essential for expressing your sense of style identity because they let you add character, originality, and personal meaning to your clothing. Accessories offer a canvas for self-expression that goes beyond apparel alone, whether it's the appeal of jewelry, the classic beauty of hats and headwear, or the skill of picking the right handbag. As you delve deeper into the world of accessories, you'll discover that you've opened up a world of limitless possibilities, each well-chosen item enriching your fashion adventure.

# 34. The Art of Scarves: Stylish and Versatile Accessorizing Ideas

One of the most adaptable and transformational accessories, scarves can give your clothes a dash of class, coziness, and personality. Whether you're going for casual chic or sophisticated elegance, the art of scarf accessorizing allows you to explore a variety of unique and fashionable ways to enhance your outfits.

## 34.1 Different Scarf Types

### 34.1.1 Classic Silk Scarves

Silk scarves can be tied to your handbag, draped around your neck, or even made into a headband. They emanate an enduring air of elegance.

### 34.1.2 Cozy blanket scarves

During the winter months, blanket scarves offer warmth and comfort. They can also be draped, wrapped, or belted to make a fashionable statement.

### 34.1.3 Scarves with loops and infinity

With its looped pattern, infinity scarves offer a casually stylish appearance that can be placed over many different outfits.

### 34.1.4 Beach scarves and sarongs

Sarongs and beach scarves, which may be worn as cover-ups, skirts, or even dresses, are ideal for vacation styling.

## 34.2 Techniques for Styling

### 34.2.1 Neckbands and Wraps

Try out various neck wraps and knots to get a variety of appearances, from casual and carefree to polished and well-knotted.

### 34.2.2 The Belted Scarf

Dresses, tunics, and baggy shirts will gain shape and dimension when you turn your scarf into a fashionable belt.

### 34.2.3 Turbans and head coverings

Turbans and head wraps can elevate your appearance and give your hair a boho or vintage feel.

### 34.2.4 Scarf as a Topper

Add a touch of class and sophistication to your outfit by wrapping a scarf around your shoulders and wearing it as a shawl or cape.

# 35. Shoe Symphony: Finding the Perfect Pair of Heels and Flats

Every ensemble starts with shoes since they anchor your appearance while also making a statement about your personal style. In the search for the ideal pair, it's important to take comfort and usefulness into account in addition to looks to make sure your footwear choice matches your clothing and way of life.

## 35.1 Important Shoe Designs

### 35.1.1 Traditional ballet shoes

Ballet flats elegantly transition from casual to dressy settings while providing enduring elegance and comfort.

### 35.1.2 Sleek Loafers

An elegant and functional choice for both business clothes and weekend trips is loafers.

### 35.1.3 Statement heels

Statement heels give your outfit a bit of glitz and instantly enhance your confidence for important occasions.

### 35.1.4 Relaxed Sneakers

Sneakers combine fashion and comfort, allowing you to add an athletic edge to your athleisure and casual attire.

## 35.2 Shoe Choices for Various Outfits

### 35.2.1 Day-to-Day Comfort

For daily tasks, choose supportive footwear that is comfortable and that doesn't restrict your movement.

### 35.2.2 Improving Casual Clothing

To create a casual, laid-back style, wear sneakers or ballet flats with jeans, dresses, or skirts.

### 35.2.3 Elegant Business Clothes

Choose slick loafers or heels that will complement your business dress and radiate professionalism.

### 35.2.4 Elegant Nights

Your evening clothes are elevated by statement heels or chic sandals, which offer a dash of appeal and sophistication.

## 35.3 Shoe Comfort and Care

### 35.3.1 Correct Sizing and Fit

To avoid discomfort and foot-related problems, make sure your shoes fit comfortably and offer enough support.

### 35.3.2 Shoe maintenance

To extend the life and preserve the appearance of your shoes, clean, polish, and protect them on a regular basis.

### 35.3.3 Cushioning and Insoles

When wearing shoes with little cushioning, increase comfort by adding insoles and cushioning for more support.

### 35.3.4 Rotation and variety

Rotate your shoe selections to give your feet varied amounts of support and prevent excessive wear on a single pair.

You develop the ability to add texture, color, and individuality to your ensembles as you learn the art of scarves and start a shoe symphony. Shoes anchor your style and serve as the basis for your entire look, while scarves serve as a magical canvas for your creativity. You may improve your accessorizing abilities and make each outfit a harmonious symphony of components that reflect your individual fashion sensibility by experimenting with different scarf style techniques and choosing the ideal pair of shoes for any situation.

# Part IX: Embracing Personal Expression

Your choice of dress as a woman provides a potent platform for expressing your uniqueness, self-assurance, and cultural background. This part explores the core of personal expression and invites you to consider how your sense of style may serve as a platform for showcasing your true self and paying respect to your cultural heritage.

# 36. Tapping into Your Inner Muse: How to Dress with Confidence and Authenticity

A profound voyage of self-discovery, dressing with confidence and authenticity allows you to use clothing's transformative ability to represent your inner essence and desires. By following your individual inspiration, you may transcend fads and social conventions to design looks that speak to your soul and exude steadfast confidence.

**36.1 Aligning Your Inner Muse at**

### 36.1.1 Being True to Yourself

Whether you are drawn to bright colors, delicate fabrics, or edgy styles, choose clothing items that reflect your personality qualities.

### 36.1.2 Accepting Symbols and Motifs

Include symbols, motifs, or patterns that have special meaning for you or express messages consistent with your ideals.

### 36.1.3 Using Clothes to Empower

You can empower yourself by dressing yourself in items that make you feel good about yourself and give you confidence.

## 36.2 Designing Signature Styles

### 36.2.1 The Influence of Dress Codes

Create a signature look by adopting a uniform look that makes getting dressed every day easier and highlights your uniqueness.

Statement pieces as forms of expression 36.2.2

Make a statement with bold accessories or distinctive clothing to express your sense of fashion and your personal beliefs.

### 36.2.3 Depth-based layering

To create multi-dimensional ensembles that highlight your inventiveness and range of personal expression, layer several pieces of clothes.

### 36.3 Milestones for Dressing for Life

### 36.3.1 Honoring Successes

Choose costumes that honor your successes and anniversaries so that they can act as a visual reminder of your path.

### 36.3.2 Adapting to Change

Utilize clothing as a vehicle for opening new chapters in your life by changing your style to match the changes and transitions you are experiencing.

## 37. Honoring Cultural Traditions: Combining History with Modern Design

Your cultural background is a rich tapestry of customs, ideals, and aesthetics that can be incorporated into your modern wardrobe. By embracing cultural customs, you may honor your roots while putting together ensembles that connect the past and the present, giving your style a distinctive and alluring look.

### 37.1 Honoring Cultural Aspects

#### 37.1.1 Traditional Textiles

Add traditional textiles to contemporary attire, including handwoven fabrics or elaborate needlework.

#### 37.1.2 Traditional Motifs

Consider including folkloric motifs and patterns in your clothing to add a sense of legacy. These elements should be indicative of your culture.

### 37.1.3 Modernizing Classic Clothing

Put a modern spin on classic clothing by adding fashionable accessories or wearing a traditional skirt with a contemporary shirt.

## 37.2 Fusion of cultures

### 37.2.1 International Inspiring

Create a distinctive fusion style by drawing influence from numerous civilizations and incorporating features from various traditions.

### 37.2.2 Cross-Cultural Accessories

To honor diversity, accessorize your clothing with items from several cultures, such as jewelry, scarves, or headpieces.

### 37.2.3 Cultural Homage of the Present

By combining traditional hues, patterns, or items into your everyday wardrobe, you can pay homage to your cultural background.

## 37.3 Cultural sensitivity and respect

### 37.3.1 Recognizing Cultural Importance

To ensure courteous and well-informed styling, educate yourself on the cultural significance of various clothing items and accessories.

### 37.3.2 Keeping Away From Cultural Appropriation

When incorporating cultural characteristics, use tact and make sure to respect and honor rather than appropriate or stereotypical.

### 37.3.3 Fashion as a Vehicle for Cultural Dialogue

Through your dress choices, start important discussions about cultural history to promote appreciation and understanding.

You start a profoundly enlightening journey of personal expression by embracing your cultural roots and following your inner creativity. Your style is wholly your own since it reflects your values, aspirations, and sense of cultural pride to the outside world. Your wardrobe becomes a canvas for painting the portrait of your vivid, self-assured, and culturally rooted self, whether you're creating hallmark styles that represent your character or fusing legacy with contemporary style.

# 38. Custom Creations: Designing Your Own Clothing and Accessories

A magnificent voyage of creativity and self-expression is creating your own clothes and accessories. By taking control of the fashion design process, you can create one-of-a-kind items that reflect your sense of fashion, character, and creative vision. This chapter goes into the world of custom designs, giving you the tools you need to realize your aspirations in the fashion industry.

## 38.1 Examining DIY Clothing

### 38.1.1 Unleashing Your Creativity

As you play around with different fabrics, colors, and materials to bring your creations to life, embrace the joy of crafting.

### 38.1.2 Repurposing and Remodeling

Old clothes can be given a fresh look by adding details, changing silhouettes, or combining different items.

### 38.1.3 Craftsmanship in Accessories

Create unique accessories, such as jewelry, hairstyles, and purses, to complete your looks and highlight your creativity.

## 38.2 Creating Clothing Designs

### 38.2.1 Planning and Sketching

Create thorough blueprints to help you through the creation process and use sketches to help you visualize your concepts.

### 38.2.2 Creating Patterns

To ensure that your clothes fit and drapes wonderfully on your body, learn the craft of pattern-making.

### 38.2.3 Construction and Sewing

Learn how to sew to make your designs come to life, from choosing materials to stitching minute details.

## 38.3 Customizing Accessory

Beadwork and embellishments 38.3.1

For a sense of grandeur and charm, add elaborate beadwork, embroidery, or decorations to accessories.

### 38.3.2 Bold Accessories

Create bold jewelry items that highlight your artistic talent and enhance the impact of your ensemble.

### 38.3.3 Customized Purses & Bags

By choosing materials, styles, and closures that go with your distinctive sense of style, you can create bespoke handbags and clutches.

## 39. Your ongoing style evolution: The Fashion Journey

Your personal style is constantly changing and evolving as a result of your development, life experiences, and shifting viewpoints. You have the knowledge to adjust to new trends, welcome changing tastes, and create a look that still accurately reflects who you are as you go off on your eternal adventure.

### 39.1 Adopting Modern Trends

### 39.1.1 Openness to Change

Keep an open mind as you research new trends in clothing and incorporate them into your personal style.

### 39.1.2 Integrating with Intention

Consider carefully whatever new trends you want to include, making sure they complement your aesthetic and personal taste.

### 39.2 Promoting Classical Elements

### 39.2.1 Specialty Items

Keep a collection of timeless pieces that serve as the foundation for your growing style.

### 39.2.2 Making Quality Investments

Make long-lasting investments in high-quality clothing and accessories to build a wardrobe of timeless elegance.

## 39.3 Accepting Life Changes

### 39.3.1 Milestone Clothing Modifications

Celebrate major life events by changing your attire to reflect your changing responsibilities, successes, and phases.

### 39.3.2 Flexibility and Adaptability

Adapt your look to suit lifestyle changes like new experiences, children, or professional changes.

## 39.4 Using clothing as a form of self-expression

### 39.4.1 Beyond Garments

Include other forms of self-expression outside clothing, such as hairstyles, cosmetics, and accessories that complement your changing sense of style.

### 39.4.2 Trust in Decisions

Regardless of what other people think or the latest trends, trust your own fashion sense and embrace your individual inclinations.

### 39.4.3 Evolution as Empowerment

Consider the development of your personal style as a potent type of self-empowerment that enables you to express yourself honestly.

You may create items that captivate your imagination and highlight your own sense of style thanks to the experience of making your own clothes and accessories. Your wardrobe develops into an evolving gallery of self-expression as your sense of style progresses, with each item representing a different stage in your development and representing your goals and desires. Celebrate the longevity of your fashion journey and the beauty of custom designs as you embrace them, understanding that your changing sense of style is an exceptional canvas on which you may create the masterpiece of your life.

# Conclusion: An Elegant and Self-Assured Journey

As we come to the end of this fascinating voyage, we ask you to take a moment to pause and consider the amazing change that has occurred within these pages. You set out on a journey of self-discovery, learning the secrets of personal style and immersing yourself in a world where clothes are an orchestra of self-expression, grace, and self-assurance. The chapters you've read are more than just words on a page; they serve as the foundation for a confident, radiant you.

You have the potential to influence how the world sees you with every decision you make, from wrist accessories to the colors that adorn your body. The art of clothing is not a frivolous activity; it is a manifestation of self-love that permeates every movement, gesture, and smile you make. You have acquired the skills necessary to create a truly you-driven style that speaks for itself before you even say a word as you have thoroughly explored each chapter.

Reader, elegance is not just found in glossy magazines or on the runways of high fashion. It's an internal state of being when your inner self and the fabric of your garment are in sync. You've developed the ability to create a sophisticated symphony with each painstakingly chosen ensemble, a song that moves to the beat of your heart. You've constructed a tapestry of beauty, adaptability, and self-assurance using versatile wardrobe basics and the art of accessorizing.

You might catch a glimpse of the person you were before this adventure started when you stand in front of your reflection. But now, that individual is adorned with fresh information, a firm sense of who they are, and a wardrobe that reflects their spirit. The days of hesitation and doubt are over because you now have the skills necessary to dress elegantly, exude confidence, and handle every situation with grace.

Our sincere hope is that you will put this information to use and grow as you become a shining example of fashion and confidence. Imagine yourself entering every room with a sense of style that begs for attention — not via showy extravagance, but rather through the calm power of self-assurance. Imagine being the center of attention at events, exuding charisma and charm as a result of the extraordinary adventure you've been on.

We invite you to share your success story as you traverse this elegant environment. Write a glowing review of this book to express how much of an influence it has made on your life. Your review will act as a beacon of hope for those who are hoping to undergo the same transition, giving them the confidence to dress stylishly and with style. Your thoughts might serve as the starting point for someone else's quest for empowerment and self-knowledge.

Finally, dear reader, keep in mind that the quest of style and self-assurance is a constant evolution rather than a destination. Accept the ever-evolving nature of style and let it reflect your development, experiences, and goals. Explore, experiment, and fine-tune your distinctive style as you go because every day is an opportunity to express the special beauty that lives within you.

We sincerely appreciate you joining us on this adventure, and we are grateful. May you walk on a path of beauty, have a heart full of self-assurance, and be led in every stride by the grace of your own special elegance. Watch yourself shine with the brilliance of a woman who knows her worth, dresses with purpose, and proudly exemplifies the art of exquisite self-expression. Dress with aim. Embrace your personality.

# HAPPY DRESSING

Made in the USA
Middletown, DE
22 August 2024